Living a Life by Design
Crafting Your Unique Success Story

Sophie Frances Patel

Table of Contents

1. Introduction 2
2. Unleashing Your Inner Potential 3
    2.1. Discovering Your Inner Reservoir 3
    2.2. The Role of Self-Belief 4
    2.3. Fueling it with Desire and Passion 4
    2.4. Strengths, Weaknesses, and the Value of Balance 4
    2.5. Nurturing Your Potential: The Habit of Lifelong Learning 5
    2.6. Uncovering Strength in Vulnerability 5
3. Mastering the Art of Self-Discovery 7
    3.1. The Power of Self-Discovery 7
    3.2. Journeys within Landscapes of Consciousness 8
    3.3. Introspection: A Key to Unlock the Inner Self 8
    3.4. Understanding and Embracing Uniqueness 9
4. Defining Your Unique Definition of Success 11
    4.1. Identifying Your Values 11
    4.2. Rearranging Your Priorities 11
    4.3. Crafting Your Success Metrics 12
    4.4. Embracing Evolution of Success 12
    4.5. Honoring Personal Satisfaction 13
5. Living Intentionally: Your Choices Matter 14
    5.1. The Philosophy of Intentional Living 14
    5.2. The Art of Mindful Decision-Making 15
    5.3. Embracing the Power of Choice 15
    5.4. Cultivating a Habit of Conscious Choices 16
    5.5. Constructive Decision-Making Strategies 16
6. Pillars of Personal Growth 18
    6.1. Recognizing Your Worth 18
    6.2. Cultivating Self-Awareness 19

- 6.3. Nurturing Emotional Intelligence ... 19
- 6.4. Embracing Lifelong Learning ... 20
- 7. Drawing Your Blueprint: Strategies for a Life by Design ... 22
  - 7.1. Foundational Principles for Designing Your Life ... 22
  - 7.2. Crafting Your Vision ... 22
  - 7.3. Setting Your Goals ... 23
  - 7.4. Developing Your Action Plan ... 23
  - 7.5. Monitoring and Adjusting Your Path ... 24
- 8. Overcoming Obstacles: Turn Trials into Triumphs ... 25
  - 8.1. Embracing Obstacles as Catalysts to Growth ... 25
  - 8.2. Building a Resilient Mindset ... 25
  - 8.3. Strategies to Overcome Obstacles ... 26
  - 8.4. Transmuting Trials into Triumphs ... 27
  - 8.5. Celebrating Victories: Large or Small ... 27
- 9. Embracing Change and Cultivating Resilience ... 29
  - 9.1. Embracing Change ... 29
  - 9.2. Cultivating Resilience ... 30
- 10. The Power of Networking and Mentorship ... 32
  - 10.1. The Essence of Networking ... 32
  - 10.2. The Virtue of Effective Communication in Networking ... 33
  - 10.3. The Significant Role of Mentorship ... 33
  - 10.4. The Dynamics of a Mentor-Mentee Relationship ... 33
  - 10.5. The Interplay of Networking and Mentorship ... 34
  - 10.6. The Long Road Ahead ... 34
- 11. Crafting and Celebrating Your Unique Success Story ... 36
  - 11.1. From Dream to Reality ... 36
  - 11.2. Celebrating the Wins, Big and Small ... 37
  - 11.3. Gathering the Nuggets of Wisdom ... 37
  - 11.4. Resilience: Your Secret Weapon ... 37
  - 11.5. Every Story is Unique ... 38

The only person you are destined to become is the person you decide to be.

— Ralph Waldo Emerson

Chapter 1. Introduction

Welcome to this vibrant and inspiring Special Report, "Living a Life by Design: Crafting Your Unique Success Story!". In this enthralling guide, we will be embarking on an awe-inspiring journey to the heart of your life's potential. Packed with insight-drenched tips, fascinating success stories, and compact wisdom capsules, this report serves as a stepping stone to carving out your path purposefully in the world. With a strong focus on self-discovery, intentional decision-making, and nurturing personal growth, this guide will kindle a fresh desire to craft your unique success narrative. Put your explorer's hat on; this is not just another report—it's an invitation to a riveting adventure towards building the life of your dreams. Excited? We thought so!

Chapter 2. Unleashing Your Inner Potential

The journey towards leading a life by design begins with the essential, yet often overlooked, exercise of exploring within. Within each of us is a deep reservoir of untapped potential that waits to manifest in myriad ways that enrich our life and contribute to the world around us. To ignite the flame of possibility and furnish the canvas of life with the hues of our unique capabilities, talents, and interests, we must first unleash this inner potential.

2.1. Discovering Your Inner Reservoir

Often, we embark on countless expeditions to the farthest corners of the world in search of knowledge, wisdom, and experiences to enrich our lives. Yet, one of the most profound journeys is the one that begins from within. Inside each of us is a reservoir teeming with untapped potential, inspired ideas, and prodigious capabilities. We possess an innate capacity for creativity, problem-solving, resilience, and empathy. Tapping into your inner potential requires dedicated introspection, self-awareness, and continuous learning.

The initial steps towards discovering your inner capabilities begin with acknowledging your innate talents and interests. Take time to reflect on the activities that come naturally to you, the ones you find enjoyable and where you lose track of time—the so-called flow state. Is it when you're engrossed in a mathematical problem? Or perhaps when you're tending to the needs of others, feeling a deep sense of satisfaction in seeing their wellbeing improve? The moments when you're most engaged and fulfilled offer a gateway to your underlying potential.

2.2. The Role of Self-Belief

Believing in oneself forms a crucial aspect of unleashing your potential. Self-doubt and fear of failure often hold us back from trying new things and exposing the talents that lie dormant. Recognize and confront these inhibiting feelings, reflecting on past successes and growth moments to bolster your confidence. Embrace a growth mindset, understanding that setbacks and challenges are part of the journey towards skill expansion and talent discovery. Each hurdle is an opportunity for learning and growth, not a determinant of your worth or ability.

2.3. Fueling it with Desire and Passion

Your deeply held desires and passions can act as powerful propellants, driving you towards maximizing your potential. Often, people fail not due to lack of ability but because of the missing element of passion. If you are disinclined towards what you are doing, it can lead to a lack of motivation that impedes you from realizing your full potential. On the contrary, if you are passionate about what you're doing, it fuels your drive, pushing you to leverage your skills, pushing your boundaries, and achieving great feats.

2.4. Strengths, Weaknesses, and the Value of Balance

In your endeavors to unlock your inner potential, it is imperative to maintain a balanced perspective about your strengths and weaknesses. Introspecting about your strengths can cultivate confidence, while understanding your weaknesses can create opportunities for growth and learning. Embrace your strengths as the superpowers that set you apart, and perceive your weaknesses not as flaws or obstructions, but as areas for improvement. Balancing the scales between your strengths and weaknesses, while being able to leverage them in appropriate contexts, can immensely enhance your journey towards unleashing your inner potential.

2.5. Nurturing Your Potential: The Habit of Lifelong Learning

Potential, like any other form of wealth, grows when nurtured. Adopting the habit of lifelong learning can keep your mind agile and open to possibilities. This practice entails more than just formal education—it includes self-directed learning, reading, engaging in intellectually stimulating conversations, and staying open to different life experiences. Encourage curiosity and foster an openness to learning, for these attributes invite opportunities for growth and self-improvement that result in maximizing your potential.

2.6. Uncovering Strength in Vulnerability

In the pursuit of discovering your potential, acknowledge the power of vulnerability. Vulnerability is often connoted negatively, as it exposes us to the risk of being emotionally hurt. However, it is through vulnerability that we can connect with our innermost feelings and confront our fears. By cultivating the courage to face these fears, we can push past the self-imposed boundaries that have confined our potential. This can lead to a profound understanding and acceptance of ourselves, empowering us to step out of our comfort zones and fully actualize our potential.

In this quest of unleashing your inner potential, remember that the road may twist and curve, filled with unexpected detours and steep slopes. Yet, it's these very challenges and experiences that shape, refine, and enhance the immense power within you. Strive not for perfection but for continuous growth and improvement. Embrace the journey and let the process of revealing your potential fill you with a sense of accomplishment and joy. Cherish the freedom that comes with being the author of your life's narrative, script your unique success story, and witness the dawn of an enriching life lived by design.

Chapter 3. Mastering the Art of Self-Discovery

The voyage to self-mastery begins with an inward voyage - a journey of uncovering the depths of our inner selves, learning about our quirky idiosyncrasies, hidden passions, latent talents, and above all, a cardinal understanding of our intrinsic nature.

3.1. The Power of Self-Discovery

This sub-chapter aims to illuminate the essence of self-discovery, reflecting on its significance in the grand scheme of life. To embark on this venture is to accept an open invitation to an intimate tête-à-tête with our deepest selves, facilitating an opportunity for introspection which, in turn, identifies our strengths, quirks, abilities, and aspirations. Self-discovery is largely a process of exploration, offering a treasure trove of enlightening experiences that pave the way for self-improvement, thus nudging us closer to the life we envisage living.

Deep diving into one's consciousness is not merely a pursuit of the curious; it holds enormous potential in refining every facet of our existence. The intimate familiarity with self propels us to leap beyond our confines, propelling personal and professional transformations. Irrespective of our external contexts, this power of discernment about our inner selves helps build resilience against life's tribulations, and directs our lives purposefully, fostering a more fulfilled and meaningful existence.

3.2. Journeys within Landscapes of Consciousness

Momentous discoveries await those intrepid travelers who dare to wander through the landscapes of their conscious and subconscious mind, with no mountain too high or valley too deep. They unearth buried passions, latent talents, and identify the fears that anchor their sojourns. Navigating these inner landscapes calls for honesty, curiosity, and a certain braveness to wrestle with the dragons within. It's about acknowledging the existence of these dragons — our deepest fears and insecurities — and then learning to dance with them, to understand and eventually tame our thoughts and emotions to live wholesomely and authentically. It's like a solitary walk down a labyrinth where every turn uncovers a new facet of the self, decoding the grand puzzle that is our human existence.

3.3. Introspection: A Key to Unlock the Inner Self

Our lives often resemble frenzied dances in rhythm with society's cacophony. Amid these choreographed steps, silent whispers from within yearn for our attention. Heeding these can lead us to our purest truths, tucked away in the fabric of our souls. Introspection, used as a structured, intentional process, serves as a trusted road map that guides us through the voyage of self-discovery and prompts meaningful conversations with the self.

Practicing introspection requires solitude and silence, offering ourselves a safe haven from the outside world's babbling noise and demands. Essential introspective practices include meditation, mindfulness, maintaining personal journals, and other self-reflective activities, and are crucial markers along the path to self-discovery. These practices imbibe the power to form profound connections with our thoughts, emotions, decision-making processes, and inner narratives, hence growing our self-awareness.

3.4. Understanding and Embracing Uniqueness

Understanding the need for celebrating our individuality requires the realization that no two journeys can ever mirror one another. Each individual, a meticulously crafted piece of art, distinctively unique from the rest of the world. Our personalities, life experiences, and perspectives amalgamate into this splendid masterpiece called self.

Exploring, understanding, and subsequently embracing these facets break homogeneity's shackles, creating a vibrant mosaic of our unique quirks and qualities instead. This understanding prods us gently towards an acceptance of our genuine selves, sans the desire to blend seamlessly into societal norms and expectations. Consequently, the resultant authenticity fuels our growth and success across personal and professional arenas.

As we unfurl the pages of the self-discovery narrative, we initiate the journey of a lifetime that leads us towards a far more qualitative, fruitful, and fulfilled version of our existence. Authenticity, born out of discovery and understanding of the self, becomes our compass, perennially guiding and ensuring an alignment with our innermost values, aspirations, and dreams. Thus, the art of self-discovery encompasses understanding the layers of our consciousness, reflecting upon our intrinsic attributes through introspection, and wholeheartedly embracing our uniqueness as we stride towards crafting our unique success stories.

And as we persistently navigate on this path, embarking on this illuminating odyssey, we kindle a newfound love for the voyage itself, understanding that truth is successive, and self-discovery perpetual. Bonding with our inner selves, we come to realize that the real triumph lies not in the destination, but in the joy of the journey and the enriching experiences along the way.

Chapter 4. Defining Your Unique Definition of Success

Before diving headlong into a journey of creating your unique life by design, it is crucial to understand the landmark which will guide the entire journey—success. What does success mean? For some, it might signify clinching that elusive promotion at work or earning a six-figure salary, driving the latest sports car or owning an enormous mansion on the hills. For others, success could entail a giggle-infested family dinner, tranquility in the heart, or contributing to society. Our society often feeds us a standard template of success—wealth, power, fame, and beauty. But is this universal definition relevant to everyone? Most definitely not! Your definition of success is just as unique as your fingerprint. Therefore, crafting your unique definition of success forms the cornerstone upon which your life by design will rest.

4.1. Identifying Your Values

To chisel your unique definition of success, it is pivotal to uncover the deep-seated values that guide your thoughts, actions, and decisions. Is their respect, affection, freedom, peace, or integrity? Your values are your compass in this vast ocean of life, steering you in the direction of what you deem as important and gratifying.

Make a list of your top five values and mull over how they connect with your definition of success. Imbuing your life with these core values can indeed be a facet of your unique success.

4.2. Rearranging Your Priorities

Equally critical to establishing your unique definition of success is rearranging your priorities. Life pulls us in a million different directions, but what are the elements that make you feel alive, fulfilled, and content? Is it spending quality time with your family, building your business empire, volunteering at a local charity, or perhaps, learning a new language?

Arrange your life's many facets by the order of priority, and you will unmask the key aspects you wish to excel in, thereby aiding you in sculpting your definition of success.

4.3. Crafting Your Success Metrics

Once you ignite the flame of self-understanding about your values and priorities, the next step is to craft your success metrics. These are the concrete milestones or evidence that you have trailblazed on your unique path to success.

Do not limit your success metrics to monetary gains. They could range from leading a balanced life, finding your purpose, expanding your comfort zone, nurturing relationships, or even overcoming fear. Remember, these personal milestones are exclusive to you and demonstrate how far you have come on your unique journey.

To help construct these metrics, list your goals as per their importance, draft an action plan to reach them, and celebrate when you tick each one off. Physical evidence of your success adds a dollop of motivation, propelling you further towards your designated finish line.

4.4. Embracing Evolution of Success

As you progress along your journey, recognize that your definition of success isn't etched in stone. It's malleable and will evolve with your growth. Stick your ear against its rhythmic heartbeat—redefine it, refine it, and let it be as fluid as your experiences, lessons, and transformations.

Keep reassessing your values, priorities, and success metrics, ensuring that they resonate with your true self at any given point in your journey. The ascension of such a continually evolving definition is indeed a reflection of your growth and an inherent part of your unique success story.

4.5. Honoring Personal Satisfaction

Finally, the keystone in defining your unique success should be your personal satisfaction. A life lived according to others' terms, chasing someone else's dreams, will merely leave you feeling empty. Rather, relish in the joy of aligning your actions with your values, priorities, and desires. Regardless of external acknowledgments, the giddy fizz of excitement you feel in your heart when carrying out tasks aligned with your version of success should be your guiding light.

Though counterintuitive, the concept of success is subjective, not objective. The societal definition of success need not necessarily resonate with you, and that's perfectly fine. You are the magisterial author and audacious hero of your unique story—the success chapter can only be penned by you.

Chapter 5. Living Intentionally: Your Choices Matter

Living intentionally is not a momentary choice—it's a lifestyle. It is the conscious decision to seize every moment, staying true to your purpose and actively making decisions to further your journey towards the life you've designed. Your choices matter—they can either steer you towardsor away from your desired path. However, before we delve deeper into this concept, let's first establish the philosophical underpinnings that foster the culture of living intentionally.

5.1. The Philosophy of Intentional Living

At its core, intentional living advocates embracing the decision-making power we wield over our lives. It is an antidote to the societal pressure of living life 'by default'—following predetermined norms or swimming aimlessly with the current of life's random circumstances. Your life is a sprawling canvas, and you hold the palette to paint it vibrant with purposeful choices.

Because every choice is the raw material from which your life story is crafted, selecting mindfully doesn't mean merely ticking off a laundry list of goals. It encompasses a broader perspective, echoing the eloquence of famed philosopher Socrates, who asserted, "An unexamined life is not worth living."

Examining life demands a constant interplay of introspection, evaluation, and adjustment, all of which ground you firmly in the present moment and acquaint you with the intrinsic power of choice.

It further involves aligning your decisions with values, understanding their potential impact, and assuming responsibility for the outcomes.

5.2. The Art of Mindful Decision-Making

Let's now explore the concept of mindful decision-making, a cornerstone of intentional living. It's an exercise where every choice, big or small, aligns with your overarching life goals and personal values, acting as a stepping-stone towards your life by design.

This synergy between choices and goals underlines the importance of living in alignment with your heart and mind. When your choices resonate with your inner self, you create an invincible harmony that fuels your journey forward.

To accomplish this, set aside quiet moments for contemplation. Regularly evaluate your objectives, reflect on options, and consider the effects of your decisions. You need not rush; slow down and take time. Aided by self-awareness and clarity of intent, let your insights guide your choices.

5.3. Embracing the Power of Choice

The power of choice affects all aspects of your life, from your mental state to your physical wellbeing, relationships, career, and overall life trajectory. Understanding this power is a crucial step towards intentional living.

Instead of allowing external circumstances to dictate your life, harness the power of conscious decision-making to shape it as you see fit. Trivial as some choices may seem, remember: even a small pebble can cause massive ripples in a serene pond.

Embrace the role of a proactive life-architect and not a passive bystander. Let your choices, not circumstances, define your reality. This doesn't mean you can control everything; it's about taking charge of what's within your realm of influence.

5.4. Cultivating a Habit of Conscious Choices

Cultivating a habit of conscious choices involves a disciplined mind and a receptive emotional state. It demands you take stock of your current reality while daring to envision a preferred future.

Begin by acknowledging that every choice matters, and practice mindfulness in action. Deeply attuned to your thoughts and feelings, you'll cultivate a holistic understanding of your decision-making process.

Consider various possibilities and potential outcomes of your choices. Your internal feedback will become amplified, enabling you to make decisions salient to your unique success story.

Create a feedback loop to evaluate—and reevaluate—your decisions. Learn from your triumphs and missteps while appreciating the wisdom each experience offers. Adopt a growth mindset, welcoming every opportunity to expand your horizon as you carve your path purposefully.

5.5. Constructive Decision-Making Strategies

Having underscored the significance of conscious decisions, let's outline some constructive decision-making strategies.

- **Embrace uncertainty**: Accept that you can't predict all outcomes. Comfort with uncertainty grants you the courage to make decisions without fear.

- **Align with personal values**: When choices align with your values and life goals, decision-making becomes less stressful.
- **Thoughtful reflection**: Engage in proactive reflection. Ponder the potential implications of your decisions.
- **Practise patience**: Hastiness often leads to superficial evaluation. Allow ideas to simmer in your mind; give yourself the space to think deeply.
- **Learn from mistakes**: Every decision teaches something. Embrace your mistakes as stepping-stones towards better choices in the future.

Living intentionally paints your life with broad strokes of fulfilment, infusing your days with purpose, meaning, and deep-seated contentment. When you approach your life as an ongoing masterpiece, each choice becomes an thoughtful brushstroke on the canvas of your unique path. Remember, it's a continuous journey. Start now and progress gradually. Patience, persistence, and purposefulness will lead the way. By choosing mindfully, you're crafting the narrative of your life—your unique success story.

Chapter 6. Pillars of Personal Growth

Personal growth—a transformative pursuit that inspires continuous learning and introspection, crucial for constructing a frame of mind reminiscent of the oak's resilience amidst life's unpredictable weather. Amidst the bustling symphony of your life's events, honing your personal growth pillars is nonnegotiable, painting a clear portrait of your destiny in the canvas of reality. And where, you may ask, lies the starting point of this voyage into the essence of personal growth?

6.1. Recognizing Your Worth

Firstly, it is fundamentally true that our personal journeys of growth and development must originate from a point of self-recognition and appreciation. The acceptance—and celebration—of your self-worth serves as the sturdy foundation upon which your unique mantelpiece of growth and success is built. Affirming your worth is an antidote to self-doubt, insecurity, and the stifling fear of failure. Just as a flower cannot bloom without first embracing its core of existence, you cannot pursue comprehensive personal growth without recognizing your inherent worth.

Take a moment to look within and affirm that you are deserving of growth, success, and happiness. It is often simple to measure our worth against societal standards or peer comparisons. But remember, your worth is immutable and cannot be defined externally—it is an inherent trait that you possess simply by being. You are not an idle cog in the sprawling machine of existence; you are a dynamic, central player in the grand theatre of life. Embrace this reality!

6.2. Cultivating Self-Awareness

Cultivating self-awareness is a cardinal pillar of personal growth. It involves the conscious practice of observing one's thoughts, emotions, behaviors, and responses to different life situations. This self-inquiry propels towards a clearer understanding of one's strengths, weaknesses, values, motivations, and desires—forging the vital roadmap for personal growth.

Think about it as embarking on an expedition through the vast expanses of your psyche. Each journey you undertake strengthens your awareness of who you are and what moves you, freeing you to make more deliberate choices that align with your personal growth ambitions.

Self-awareness allows you to identify areas in your life requiring improvement or transformation, providing the impetus for cultivating new habits, acquiring new skills, or making a significant life-altering decision. Understand that you are a constant work in progress, and each moment offers yet another opportunity to embrace growth.

6.3. Nurturing Emotional Intelligence

A critical cornerstone shoring up the edifice of personal growth is the capacity for emotional intelligence. This competency enables you to understand, use, and manage your emotions in positive ways to relieve stress, communicate effectively, empathize with others, overcome challenges, and defuse conflict.

Imagine on a rainy day when clouds screen the sun's radiant beams. Instead of becoming frustrated with the weather, you perceive the rain's therapeutic patter, savoring the calming ambiance it engenders. That's emotional intelligence in action—it allows you to pick out the sun behind the stormy clouds of every situation.

Emotional intelligence enhances self-awareness, fostering empathy and strengthening interpersonal relationships—it is a powerful tool aiding you in navigating the multifaceted human experience. Emotional intelligence is not just about achieving personal milestones but also about generating meaningful connections and fostering a harmonious coexistence with others—a vital pedal rotating the wheel of personal growth.

6.4. Embracing Lifelong Learning

Finally, the practice of lifelong learning is a compelling pillar of personal growth. In an ever-evolving world, the only constant is change. To adapt and excel in such dynamic times, you must dedicate yourself to constant learning and unlearning.

Whether it's learning a new language, mastering a musical instrument, exploring advanced technology, or understanding human psychology, your commitment to learning new skills and concepts contributes significantly to your personal development trajectory. Not only does it improve your competence, but it also keeps your brain active and engaged, enhancing cognitive functioning and mental health.

Lifelong learning should not be taken as a strenuous exercise, but rather as a thrilling journey to broaden horizons, satisfy curiosity, and discover new facets of life. Choose to perceive the unknown not as a graveyard of fears, but as a garden blooming with opportunities for growth and wisdom.

In this vibrant symphony of life, you are your own composer, charged with harmonizing the notes of self-worth, self-awareness, emotional intelligence, and lifelong learning to create the stirring melody of personal growth. Every day presents a fresh set of measures on your composition sheet. How you choose to arrange the notes within these blocks will determine the rhythm and melody of your life's composition. Embrace each day as a momentous opportunity to deepen your understanding of yourself and the world around you. As you thread this path, remember to pause, reflect and celebrate your journey as you evolve into the best version of yourself!

Chapter 7. Drawing Your Blueprint: Strategies for a Life by Design

Drawing your life blueprint is akin to an architect designing a magnificent building. Just as the building starts with an ambitious vision, committed planning, and precise execution, so does the design of your life. Detailed considerations and strategic decisions are paramount in determining the success of this endeavor, and we shall delve into these aspects with meticulous care.

7.1. Foundational Principles for Designing Your Life

First off, bear in mind that your life design should reflect your own unique blend of hopes, aspirations, strengths, and values. The most successful life blueprints are underscored by a firm foundation of self-awareness and authenticity. To begin with, take some time to introspect and glean valuable insights about yourself. What makes you come alive? What fuels your passion? What values guide your actions? The answers to these questions will aid you in establishing the pillars upon which you will build your life blueprint.

Moreover, your life design must be resilient enough to withstand unexpected gusts of life. Unpredicted events may sometimes divert your course, but the sturdiness of your life blueprint should allow for reiterations when circumstances demand.

7.2. Crafting Your Vision

In order to forge a path towards a life by design, you must first craft a compelling vision. Start by envisioning where you want to be in your life some years from now. This is not just about financial or social status but extends to all aspects of life including health, relationships, and personal development. Your vision should be vivid enough to navigate you through the various paths that life presents.

Your vision serves as a compass, guiding you towards your authentic self. It's vital to revisit your vision regularly, tweaking it when necessary. A dynamic vision will always ensure that it reflects your evolving self, keeping you connected with your aspirations and dreams.

7.3. Setting Your Goals

Once your vision is firmly established, you can move on to setting your goals. Goals are the milestones that will ultimately lead you to your envisioned future. These could be short-term or long-term goals, set for various aspects of your life.

Remember, goals should be SMART - Specific, Measurable, Achievable, Relevant, and Time-bound. The SMART framework provides a structure that helps ensure your goals are clear and reachable. Each goal you set should align with your vision and bring you closer to realizing your life by design.

7.4. Developing Your Action Plan

Following the setting of your goals, an action plan is a necessary step to actualize your life blueprint. This imperative tool concretizes your path, providing detailed steps such as when, how, and what needs to be done in order to reach your goals. Each of your goals should have a corresponding action plan outlining the steps needed to achieve them.

Action plans further break down your goals into manageable chunks, preventing any overwhelming feelings that may arise from facing a large goal all at once. This ease of reality brings your blueprint to life, turning abstract goals into concrete steps.

7.5. Monitoring and Adjusting Your Path

Frequent monitoring of your journey is essential to ensure that you are on the right track towards achieving your goals. Regularly measure your progress and reflect on your actions. What is working, and what isn't? Do your actions align with your goals?

As you evaluate your position, don't shy away from making necessary adjustments to your blueprint and your path. A detour doesn't mean failure, but rather shows your capacity to adapt to changes and grow. Life rarely goes according to plan, and your ability to fluidly alter your course is a sign of resilience and flexibility, two traits highly beneficial in a life by design.

In conclusion, the process of drawing your blueprint for a life by design is an ongoing, introspective affair. It revolves around creating a vision, setting goals, formulating plans, executing actions, and continuously reviewing your progress. Although this may seem complex, remember: this intricate design is your life. It calls for attentive detail, patient construction, and a hard-set dedication to your true self. Yes, there will be challenges, and yes, changes will be inevitable. But, with each step you take, each stone you lay in this grand design, you become closer to living that fulfilling life you've always aspired to.

Chapter 8. Overcoming Obstacles: Turn Trials into Triumphs

Indeed, no journey to success can ever be entirely devoid of obstacles, but these hurdles are not the ending, far from it. Instead, they are crescendos in your symphony of success - stark disagreements that only illuminate your composition's harmonic elements.

8.1. Embracing Obstacles as Catalysts to Growth

Perhaps one of the most profound ways to frame obstacles is to see them as catalysts of growth. These aren't the inconvenient impediments standing in your way. They serve as opportunities for learning, evolving, and growing. It is by diving head-on into these obstacles and wrestling with the inherent complexity, we experience growth and development. They push the boundaries of our comfort zones, compel us to gain new skills, and challenge our preconceived notions about our capabilities. As the saying goes, what doesn't kill us only makes us stronger. Thus, overcoming obstacles requires seeing them as stepping stones for personal and professional growth, even when they seem daunting at first glance.

8.2. Building a Resilient Mindset

Resilience is the cornerstone of overcoming obstacles. The capacity to recover from adversities, to bounce back stronger and wiser – that's resilience. Resiliency is like a sturdy vessel navigating turbulent waters; it ensures that you not only stay afloat but also progress in the storm's eye. Building a resilient mindset starts with self-belief. If you believe you can overcome, then you set yourself up to receive opportunities that foster overcoming. Each setback should fuel your resolve, while every minor triumph boosts your confidence. A resilient mindset can encourage positive thinking, prompt proactive solutions, and generate a grittier work ethic. This mindset doesn't offer you an escape from difficulty; it endows you with indomitable fortitude to march through challenges with reduced anxiety and improved adaptability.

8.3. Strategies to Overcome Obstacles

Admittedly, fostering an ironclad mindset and growth perspective is a necessary precondition, but overcoming obstacles also needs tangible strategies. Let's discuss some of these strategies.

Break It Down: Eternalize the mantra of "one step at a time". Break your problem into manageable chunks. Dissect the behemoth that is your obstacle into smaller, surmountable tasks. This strategy reduces overwhelm and makes the problem-solving process less intimidating.

Seek Support: There's no rule stating that you must conquer your trials alone. Reach out to your peers, mentors, or professional help when you need it. Inviting different perspectives can provide fresh insights and practical guidance.

Learn and Adapt: Obstacle overcoming necessitates a consistent learning attitude. What lessons does your current hurdle offer? Adapt and evolve with each roadblock. Success loves those who are nimble and quick to adjust their strategies.

Take Care of Your Physical and Mental Well-being: Regular exercise, a healthy diet, ample sleep, and mindfulness practices like meditation can augment your capacity to cope with stress. Amidst the obstacle-encountering chaos, don't forget to take care of yourself.

8.4. Transmuting Trials into Triumphs

You're a sculptor, and adversities are your marble. Your resilience, strategic approach, and commitment to personal growth carve out the victorious masterpiece. With every strike of the hammer, obstacles dissolve away and successes take shape. In the grand picture, each trial serves as a critical element in your success story. The transmutation of trials into triumphs is not just about surmounting obstacles; it's more about the transformation it induces within you, the lessons it instills, the resilience it hardens, and the personal growth it sparks.

8.5. Celebrating Victories: Large or Small

Nothing nourishes the spirit like celebrating victories, both large and small. Applaud yourself for each triumph over adversity. Every problem defeated contributes significantly to your journey; thus, acknowledging these victories, however small, fuels motivation and exercises optimism. It strengthens your belief in your prowess as an obstacle conqueror, and imparts the confidence to meet future challenges with a winky smile and a winner's spirit.

To conclude, obstacles are essential parts of your life's narrative. They don't ambush on your scenic journey to success; rather, they add value and create engaging chapters. It is by overcoming these hurdles that one crafts an authentic and inspiring success saga. So, go forth and flip trials into triumphs with unyielding resilience, unwavering determination, and relentless pursuit of personal growth. Remember, in the grand design of life, obstacles are not your foes; they are the mentors instructing you, shaping you, and refining you to achieve your unique definition of success.

Chapter 9. Embracing Change and Cultivating Resilience

This enticing journey begins with a fundamental truth—change is the only constant. No matter how hard one tries to avoid it, change remains omnipresent and unavoidable. The key to navigating this flux is embracing change and cultivating resilience. This chapter will provide a detailed exploration of these ideas, helping you to become more adaptable and robust.

9.1. Embracing Change

Change comes in many forms. Sometimes it's planned, like a strategic move to a new job or city. Other times, it's unexpected, like the sudden loss of a loved one or a disruptive global event. Regardless of the nature and degree of change, our lives are continuously evolving and we must learn to grapple with, and ultimately embrace change.

The first step in embracing change is understanding that change isn't inherently negative. While it can be daunting and initially uncomfortable, change often leads to growth, development, and new possibilities. Therefore, instead of resisting it, consider reframing your perspective of change. View it as an essential part of life, filled with opportunities for evolution and improvement.

A technique to foster this perspective involves maintaining an open mind. Plan, but also create room for spontaneity and flexibility. Cultivate a readiness to challenge your comfort zone and remain open to different experiences and perspectives. This mental preparedness can transform feelings of fear or intimidation about change into anticipation and excitement about the future's potential.

Another crucial aspect is practicing acceptance. Things may not always go according to plan, and that's alright. The more quickly you can accept change, the more effectively you can adapt to it. Remember, your response to change is within your control, even when the change itself may not be.

9.2. Cultivating Resilience

While embracing change is essential, equally important is cultivating resilience— the ability to "bounce back" from adversity and maintain a positive outlook amidst challenges.

There are several paths to cultivating resilience, and they typically start with understanding and managing one's emotions. Heightened self-awareness enables you to comprehend your emotional responses to different situations better. This insight can be a powerful tool that helps manage your reactions and approach challenges from a place of inner strength and calmness.

Promoting physical wellbeing can significantly boost resilience. Ensuring a balanced diet, regular exercise, and adequate sleep can enhance physical health and mental fortitude. The connection between the mind and body should not be underrated – maintaining physical wellbeing provides a firm foundation for mental resilience.

Additionally, maintaining strong relationships can contribute to resilience. Establishing supportive connections with friends, family, and mentors can provide emotional support, diverse perspectives, and practical advice during challenging times. Remember, you don't have to navigate life's turbulence alone.

An attitude of optimism and gratitude is another fundamental facet of resilience. Practicing positive thinking and recognizing life's blessings, even amidst hardships, can fuel resilience and offer a broader perspective.

Finally, remember that cultivating resilience is an ongoing process, not a one-time event. Regularly reflect on your experiences, continue learning from challenges, and incrementally incorporate healthy coping techniques into your lifestyle.

Embracing change and cultivating resilience are not just survival tactics but pathways to a happier, more fulfilling life. As you continue your journey towards living a life by design, remember that these practices are your allies, enabling you to plot your course and navigate life's shifting tides with grace and tenacity. By learning to dance with change rather than fighting it, and by building mental and emotional buoyancy, you write your unique and beautiful success story, one life chapter at a time.

To conclude this chapter, I leave you with this thought— every change, every obstacle is an opportunity in disguise. Stay resilient, embrace the constant flux, and remember, you are the author of your life's narrative, no matter how the plot twists and turns.

Chapter 10. The Power of Networking and Mentorship

Commencing this profound exploration of the topic at hand, we will delve into the heart of two intimately intertwined aspects of a successful life - networking and mentorship. They demarcate a distinctive path lit with opportunities, insight, and growth. Both networking and mentorship are unique processes that feed into each other, thereby creating an intertwined dynamic that can significantly impact your journey to success.

10.1. The Essence of Networking

At its core, networking is about establishing connections and building mutually beneficial relationships. These relationships can extend from your professional life into personal territories. Networking, as we traditionally understand it, permeates through conferences, social events, and professional meet-ups. Still, it can also manifest in online forums, communities, and platforms.

In today's hyper-connected world, networking expands beyond the geographic boundaries, cultures, and socio-economic barriers. Leveraging digital platforms, you can engage with professionals, thought leaders, and innovators from various domains around the globe. Remember that the span of your network is directly proportional to the breadth of knowledge and perspectives you can access. Each interaction withstands the potential to catalyze new ideas, foster innovation, and instigate growth.

10.2. The Virtue of Effective Communication in Networking

Possessing several key skills can elevate your networking game. Among them, the ability to communicate effectively is paramount. Clear and concise communication coupled with active listening fosters stronger connections. Going beyond the superficial level, creating deep, meaningful interactions helps in strengthening your networking approach.

Also, it is essential to enter the networking process with the intention of giving before taking. The most nourishing relationships often emerge from the soil of generosity. Show genuine interest in others, be ready to offer help, and share knowledge or resources where possible. The law of reciprocity will ensure that you receive the same kindness in unexpected ways.

10.3. The Significant Role of Mentorship

Moving onto mentorship, we find another powerful catalyst for personal and professional development. A mentor is usually someone who has traversed down a similar path as yours, accumulating wisdom, insights, and experiences to share with you. As a more experienced guide, a mentor can assist you in navigating your journey more effectively, avoiding common pitfalls and leveraging tried-and-true strategies for success.

10.4. The Dynamics of a Mentor-Mentee Relationship

A mentor-mentee relationship isn't a one-way street. It's a dynamic partnership, a mutually responsible engagement where both parties stand to benefit. As a mentee, you gain wisdom, while, as a mentor, guiding a less experienced individual can evoke a sense of fulfillment, triggering self-reflection, and ingraining lessons more profound.

Understanding and valuing the dynamics of this relationship is an integral part of making mentorship work. The relationship thrives on trust, respect, openness, and communication. It requires an investment of time, effort, and emotional intelligence.

10.5. The Interplay of Networking and Mentorship

Now, how do networking and mentorship weave together? As you might intuit by now, networking can often be the birthplace of mentorship relationships. A network presents a broad spectrum of potential mentors to choose from.

Conversely, a mentor can open the doors to their network, providing introductions and connections that help you broaden your base. It's a symbiotic relationship where the two domains feed and thrive off each other, reinforcing the pathways to an enriching, successful life by design.

10.6. The Long Road Ahead

Thus, walking this path of networking and mentorship demands consistency, openness, and a reciprocal approach. These strategies help in expanding and diversifying your perspectives, introducing you to new ideas and opportunities, and enhancing your overall life experience.

In retrospect, networking and mentorship cannot be viewed in isolation if one seeks to craft a remarkable success story. They intertwine and interplay, each reinforcing the other, creating a resilient and robust system that amplifies personal and professional growth.

The power of networking and mentorship is all-encompassing, deeply impactful, and has the potential to dramatically alter the trajectory of one's growth journey. As you continue crafting your unique success story, remember to leverage these potent tools and cherish the enriching relationships that they beget.

Chapter 11. Crafting and Celebrating Your Unique Success Story

The concluding leg of this extraordinary journey brings us to the heartening act of crafting and celebrating your unique success story. Understanding that success is a highly personalized concept, the narratives that swirl around it naturally hold an exclusive touch as well. Integrating defining moments, overcoming challenges, and victories—both grand and small—your success story could indeed be a testament of your individuality.

11.1. From Dream to Reality

Strapped with the tools of self-discovery, clarity of personal success, intentional living, and personal growth, you now stand poised to explore the first phase of crafting your success story: Translating dreams into reality.

At times, dreams reside in the nebulous clouds of the ethereal, appearing too distant and surreal. The crux of taking them to the realm of practical, tangible reality lies in focused strategies and steadfast commitment. A helpful technique is envisioning your dream in great detail. Immerse yourself in the feeling of achieving it, let that joy fill your soul, and own that vision wholly. The vision serves as a compelling force, magnetizing each bout of effort put into achieving it.

Nestled at the heart of crafting your unique success story is the action plan. Much like an architect's plan or a filmmaker's screenplay, your life could benefit from a clear sequence of steps targeted towards your aspirations. This plan could include specific goals, milestones, or challenges anticipated, thus providing a sense of direction and momentum in your pursuit.

11.2. Celebrating the Wins, Big and Small

A pivotal aspect of crafting your success story is the recognition and celebration of victories along your path. Remember, a win does not need to be monumental to be celebrated—it could be as simple as maintaining consistency in your desired behavioral change or overcoming a minor obstacle. Celebrating small wins infuses joy into your journey and motivates you to strive for the bigger milestones.

One potent way to keep tabs on your wins is by maintaining a 'Success Journal'. Take a few minutes every day to jot down the progress you have made, the challenges you have surmounted, and the lessons you gleaned from the day.

11.3. Gathering the Nuggets of Wisdom

Every journey comes with its specific set of realizations and learnings. Make sure your success narrative is studded with such nuggets of wisdom. It's not just about the destination—it's also about the journey, and the insights gained during this process make your narrative richer and more powerful. The act of reflection, akin to mining these nuggets, brings about a deeper understanding of your growth.

11.4. Resilience: Your Secret Weapon

In the process of crafting your unique success story, you will inevitably encounter complexities, disappointments, and blocks. But remember, the strength and resilience you display in those times define your narrative as much as, if not more than, your achievements. Your story becomes one of endurance, resilience, and strength, morphing into an inspiring testament and encouraging beacon for others on a similar path.

11.5. Every Story is Unique

Finally, remember that your success story is unique to you. Just because it does not look like the societal definition or someone else's version of success, it does not rob it of its significance. The external world might have myriad opinions and standards; however, your narrative is crafted by your standards. The essence of your individual journey, punctuated by your personal growth, learnings, resilience and triumphs, renders it unique and meaningful. So dare to dream, live by design, weave your great story, and celebrate your version of success!

This chapter concludes on an uplifting note – an opportunity to rejoice and to revel in your journey. Now you are equipped with effective strategies to craft your unique success story and celebrate it, make sure to share your journey as well – we all hold the power to inspire others.

www.ingramcontent.com/pod-product-compliance
Lightning Source LLC
Chambersburg PA
CBHW070955220526
45471CB00007B/3034